# BREAKING FREE

# OF

# MANIPULATION

A STORY OF STRUGGLE

AND SURVIVAL

AFTER BEING IN THE GRIP OF A

PSYCHOPATH

**Written By**

**Melody**

I based this book on my personal experience with someone whom I believe is a psychopath. I have chosen to write using a pen name in order to protect the identity of the other individual and myself. All names mentioned herein are merely pseudonyms. The events are factual and necessary for the integrity of the book. The information disclosed is unidentifiable and mere interactions that would only be familiar to the other individual and myself and therefore will not expose or harm them in anyway. I wrote this book with the sole purpose of helping others and not with any vengeful intent.

# TABLE OF CONTENTS

A Wise Warning.................................................................. vii

Preface .......................................................................... ix

Chapter One – INTRODUCTION TO A PSYCHOPATH ..................... 1

Chapter Two - HINDSIGHT IS 20/20 .................................... 5

Chapter Three - IN THE BEGINNING: "IDEALLY HIS" ................ 17

Chapter Four – THE SLOW BOIL ........................................ 25

Chapter Five – MIND GAMES ............................................ 33

Chapter Six – PANTS ON FIRE! ........................................ 41

Chapter Seven - PRE-DISCARD/ DISCARD ............................ 45

FINAL THOUGHTS............................................................ 59

TACTICS THE PSYCHOPATH USES ALONG WITH A BRIEF DESCRIPTION............... 63

STAGES OF THE PSYCHOPATHIC BOND........................................ 67

# A Wise Warning

"A malicious man disguises himself
with his lips, but in his heart he
harbors deceit.

Though his speech is charming, do not
believe him."

Proverbs 26:24-25 NIV

# Preface

Hello Friend,

I am so pleased that you have decided to join me as we journey through my encounter with a psychopath. My experience was with a man whom I had a romantic relationship. Throughout the book, I refer to him as "Eddie." Eddie is not his real name; nor is it any part of his name. Therefore, if there are any Eddies out there reading this, rest assured, I did not write this book about you.

You will notice that I speak about psychopaths in general as male because that was the case for me. I have chosen to do so merely for convenience sake and for the sake of this writing only. I am aware that there are women psychopaths in society as well, although research seems to suggest the ratio of men to women psychopaths to be around 20:1. In no way am I minimizing the reality of the pain that women psychopaths inflict upon their victims. Moreover, not all relationships with psychopaths are romantic ones. They can be any variation of family, friends or work mates.

You may wonder if another book on psychopaths is necessary. In all of my gathering of information regarding the psychopath, I found the most comfort from those who took the time to tell their story. Therefore, I am telling my story; hoping you too will find comfort in knowing that others have been deceived by a psychopath and have come out on the other side, not only surviving but also thriving. Writing my story has also been a part of the healing process for me. Although for safety sake and anonymity I have chosen to write under a pen name, it is very liberating to be no longer afraid to disclose what took place

My hope is that you will read my story, feel validated that what is happening to you is very real, and find the courage to get the help you need to come out of the dark place you find yourself.

Believing you will,

Melody

# Chapter One – INTRODUCTION TO A PSYCHOPATH

It was cold and dark . . . lonely . . . and hopeless. There seemed no way out of the place I found myself. How did I get here? Where was I anyway? Does anyone know I am here? Is anyone even looking for me?

The air had become so heavy and oppressive I found it was becoming hard to breathe.

Desperate, I take a good look around and finally realize I am the prey caught in a spider's web. This is no ordinary web and the spider that spun it, no ordinary spider. I wanted so much to believe the sweet lies that drew me in, but now the reality of the depth of deception that was spun around me came crashing down upon me and at last I understood, the spider will return until there is nothing left of me but an empty shell.

Perhaps you have not yet become fully aware of your precarious situation; but your gut is telling you that something is not quite right. After being in the presence of a certain someone, you are left feeling confused or even angry but you are not sure why. Now, you feel guilty for even thinking such a thing!

If any of this seems familiar, you may now be or have been in the grip of a psychopath. You are not alone. I know you feel as though you are, but you are not. I repeat, "You are NOT alone."

That is what "they" want you to believe. "They" created the illusion that you are alone. "They" created the facade that there is no way out.

You may be thinking that you have nowhere to turn. No one will believe you and will probably blame you for the failure of the relationship anyway. After all, "they" are so likeable, charming, and fun. "They" have done nothing but care for you and protect you.

Besides, there were good times too … right? Maybe if you just try harder, you can regain what you first had. WRONG! Because what you first had was not real. The problem is you were dancing with the devil. It was all a lie.

"They" are psychopaths.

Contrary to popular belief, most psychopaths are not violent lunatics lurking in the shadows waiting to abduct you, take you home, chop you up and eat you for dinner.

They are your neighbors, co-workers, and acquaintances you interact with every day as you go about your life. You may even be sharing a home with a psychopath. Do not be fooled by their outward appearance or charming demeanor. You can look a psychopath right in the eye and never know their devious intentions. That is until you are in their grip and as they tighten their hold, you realize you are in a fight for your life.

The Psychopath is a chameleon, changing his or her persona at will. They are skilled manipulators who have no qualms about deceiving others in order to get what they want.

There are many misconceptions regarding the differences between psychopaths and sociopaths and quite often, these two become intertwined and mislabeled as the same disorder. To be clear, I am not an expert by any means on the topic, nor am I qualified to make a clinical diagnosis of anyone. From the research I have done, however, I have come to understand that these two differ in various ways, the most remarkable being the psychopaths' complete lack of empathy. They may act empathetic but only to blend in. If you listen closely to a psychopath feigning feelings, you can sense the shallowness of his "emotion." While sociopaths have a conscience, although admittedly a very weak one - psychopaths do not. If caught in some misdeed, a psychopath may pretend to be remorseful, but only to continue in whatever charade they have ensnared you. It is very rare for a psychopath to apologize, if ever, unless it would benefit them.

In general, high functioning psychopaths, operate covertly, and therefore are able to hide successfully their true self. Their strategies are premeditated, having taken into consideration all possible outcomes before initiating their scheme. Sociopaths on the other hand are impulsive and generally are a little easier to spot, for one, because they often have a great deal of trouble controlling their anger. Psychopaths do get angry, but on a whole, they are much smarter as to how they go about getting revenge. While the anger of a psychopath appears well controlled in public, secretly they plan to appease their anger with an attack tailored specifically for you. After the attack, others may not know who launched the strike, but you will certainly know.

Psychopaths are charming, callous, manipulative, cunning, conning, remorseless, social predators. Spider, devil, chameleon, all describe the psychopath very well. Still, the best and most accurate word to describe the psychopath, in my opinion, is PREDATOR.

The psychopath is a PREDATOR who studied you and chose YOU as their next victim.

# Chapter Two - HINDSIGHT IS 20/20

If only Eddie came with a sign flashing on his forehead, *"warning\*\*warning\*\*warning"*, I might have had a fighting chance. I say, "might" because even with many red flags, he was still able to charm his way into my life and my heart. Of course, psychopaths do not wear signs; they wear masks. Often the journey with a psychopath begins very simply as described in the two following scenes, both of which are close renditions of what actually took place.

*~Scene 1~*

Melody looked around her new office with nervous excitement. Looking at the large, round-faced clock on the wall, she realized if she did not hustle, she would be late for a meeting with the Director of Education and Training.

As she made her way swiftly down the long hallway, she could not help but notice her new co-workers. For Melody, today was an exciting new beginning; conversely, for the others she encountered, it seemed to be the same old grind. She could see it in their eyes and in the slow movement of their bodies as they trudged along carrying out their daily chores.

Distracted, she did not notice the other person as she rounded the corner until she came crashing into him, her papers spilling all over the tiled floor. Without skipping a beat, he swiftly gathered all the papers and skillfully putting them all in order, placed them into Melody's hand.

"Are you O-K?" The stranger kindly inquired.

Offering his right hand, he introduced himself, "My name is Eddie."

"My name is Melody. I am so sorry. I was not watching where I was going. I'm running late for a meeting with the Training Director."

"Please don't apologize." Then, placing both hands upon Melody's shoulders, he turned her around and pointing with his finger said, "The Training Director's office is that way."

As they headed their separate ways, Eddie called out, "If I can be of any further help to you, Melody, please let me know."

*What a nice man,* Melody thought.

*New game in town,* Eddie theorized. *I will be sure to stop by her office later today.*

## ~Scene 2~

Melody was tidying up her desk, getting ready to leave for the day, when she heard a gentle knock on the door.

Peeking inside, Eddie asks, "How's everything going?"

"Eddie! Come in!" Surprised but delighted to see him, Melody offered him a seat and cup of coffee.

*Hmmm!* Eddie considered this. *No boundaries here.*

"Did you manage to get through your first day without knocking anyone else over?" He teased.

Melody could not help but notice his smile. "I'm not normally that clumsy." She sheepishly offered as an excuse.

"So, tell me, how *was* your first day, Melody?"

"Great!" She enthusiastically blurted. As she slumped back in her chair, she added, "Overwhelming too."

*She's vulnerable . . . and trusting. Check and Check.* Eddie mentally checked off the boxes.

"You'll be fine. I can tell you are going to do great here. Promise me you will let me know if there is anything I can do to help. I'd be glad to show you the ropes."

"Eddie, that is so kind of you to offer."

"So is that a promise?"

Melody felt silly making promises to a practical stranger but at his insistence found herself saying, "I promise Eddie."

Partially out the door, Eddie turned back towards Melody and offered, "I think your office could use a fresh coat of paint. I'll make sure that happens." With a quick wink and disarming smile, off he goes.

*Wow! I cannot believe my luck in meeting such a helpful person my first day on the job!*

*Bingo!* Eddie thought with great anticipation. *My prospects just got a whole lot brighter!*

~End~

Did you catch what transpired between Melody and Eddie in those scenes? Eddie very quickly was able to ascertain Melody's trusting personality by presenting her with several opportunities to object when he crossed what others would have considered boundaries. He also was quick to note her current vulnerability and made a mental note of it, no doubt to use for his benefit. He even manipulated her into making a promise to him. While this may seem insignificant on the surface, it demonstrates how Melody was already stifling her own gut instinct and surrendering her will to him. She felt silly making the promise to him but felt compelled to do so. Eddie also was beginning to plant the idea of indebtedness to him when he offered to have her office painted. This was completely unsolicited on the part of Melody and very conniving of Eddie. In contrast to Eddie's purposeful testing of the waters and various manipulations, Melody never stopped to question why this stranger was being so overly accommodating. She naively believed that everyone is as forthright and she. Eddie, on the other hand, was wearing a mask.

The psychopaths' mask is to hide who they really are from you and their true wicked agenda for you in order to lure you into their trap. The mask is there to protect them but also serves as bait for you. They can change their mask quickly to fit any situation and any person they are currently dealing with. I only wish I had paid closer attention to my gut instinct when I witnessed Eddie's changes in persona as he sat court with the guys in the back shop, or had his giggling harem audience at the office, or as he worked his charm with the woman in customer service in order to get what he wanted. Unfortunately, by the time he allowed these other personas to surface in front of me; I truly believed that the mask he presented me was the real deal.

The Psychopath is very cunning. They have many tactics and know how and when to use them. Throughout this book, I share personal experiences and some of the tactics Eddie used on me. I have also included a list of tactics psychopaths use with brief explanations at the end of the book as a quick reference guide. I hope you find it helpful in identifying the strategies used against you.

There are three main stages in the psychopathic bond. A summary of these is also available for reference at the back of the book.

The first stage is the idealization stage in which the psychopath lures you in with their charisma, ingratiating himself to you by showering you with excessive flattery and attention. He will spend tremendous amounts of time with you. He will seduce you in such a way that you do not realize he is luring you into his trap. This is also known as love bombing because the psychopath will bomb you with absolute adulation.

During the idealization stage, Eddie had a way of making me feel so special that I would never question his love for me. He often surprised me with flowers, and I do mean surprised! One morning, I opened my front door on my way to work and a bouquet of flowers was lying on my front porch with a beautiful hand-written note telling me what a special person I was. On another occasion, I unlocked my office door and found a single flower on my chair with a homemade CD of all of our favorite love songs. Eddie also liked to bring me some of my favorite foods. After discovering we both loved the same ice cream, he would often show up at my front door with a gallon for us to enjoy, delving in together like little children with two giant spoons. At face value these appear as normal romantic gestures; however, these are only a few examples of the numerous and extravagant gestures on Eddie's part.

Once the psychopath has you hooked, and you have more than likely given him all of your love and trust, he will initiate the second stage of the psychopathic bond, called the devaluation stage. During this phase, the psychopath will begin to pull away. He will still give you small doses of positive reinforcement to keep you on the hook but he will continually push the boundaries of unacceptable behavior. As you accept the behavior he becomes less interested in you. It is a very confusing time. The mask the psychopath initially presented and wore so easily and the face you are now beginning to see do not match. This may result in a condition called cognitive dissonance. Cognitive Dissonance is an uncomfortable mental state resulting from conflicting perceptions. The "person" you first met during the idealization stage that you grew to love and trust and their new conduct contradict each other, causing a struggle within your mind.

During this time, I did not understand why I was always feeling anxious and confused. I could not really pinpoint the reason. What happened to my knight in shining armor? When I finally got up enough nerve to try to discuss it, Eddie knocked me off the pedestal he had so nicely placed me on and put me on the defensive. He made me feel as though I was crazy. Little did I realize at the time the futility of discussing this with him; after all, he purposefully created this atmosphere of ambiguity.

In fact, Eddie kept me in a <u>constant</u> state of uncertainty in order to give himself control and power over me. He rarely gave me a straight answer, even to the most basic question; he was extremely vague about everything; he often answered a question with a question; and he would not commit, even to a specific time for an outing together. He would often "disappear" for days or weeks at a time. Over time, I became unsure of myself, my relationship with him, my environment, and my future. He was a master at causing me to doubt myself and thereby the reality of his abuse. Eventually, Eddie was successful in convincing me that he was not abusive to me at all and that it was merely a perception I had formed because of my past experiences.

Because I did not know when Eddie would appear, I had to be "ready" all the time. I tried to rationalize with him that this was not only impractical, but also rude and selfish. His comeback reply was that I was the one with the problem. He would then call me "up-tight" and "controlling" for expecting him to commit himself in such a way. Occasionally, I was able to get Eddie to commit to a specific time; but he always was certain to come late. By late, I mean an hour or more late. He would arrive at my home and gleefully announce that he stopped and got a haircut or cleaned out his car "for me." (*Was I supposed to thank him for that?*) This happened often and on one occasion I asked him if he was purposefully late to annoy me. He "answered" my question by asking me a question, "Why do you always have to over-analyze everything?" I have come to learn that this is a common statement from psychopaths to their victims. If you try to bring up a topic that they do not want you broaching, they will turn the tables back on you. The psychopath does not want you to analyze them or the relationship, so they put you on the defensive with this statement, attempting to impress upon you that you are the one with the problem and ultimately you back down.

As soon as the psychopath has taken what they want and has no more use for you, they will initiate the discard stage, which is the third and final stage of the psychopathic bond. In reality, however, the psychopath has not bonded with you at all. The psychopath is incapable of truly bonding with another person. They have objectified you. You were the _object_ of their affection. More than likely they have found a new and exciting object to begin the psychopathic cycle with. I did not understand what Eddie meant at the time but I remember him saying that he wanted to fold me up and put me in his pocket and take me home so that he could take me out and play with me anytime he wanted to. Now I understand that I was nothing more than an object to amuse him.

Sadly, looking back, I relived the idealization, devaluation, and discard cycle repeatedly. I kept holding onto the hope that the man I first met would somehow miraculously reappear. Of course he never did because he never existed. Even now, 15 months later at this writing, I still have to fight the urge of falling into that trap. My mind and my intuition have two competing beliefs; I remember the euphoria of being swept off my feet, but now am experiencing pain. It is very important to recognize what is happening and understand the futility of trying to reconcile the two. The words spoken and the promises made by your psychopath were not true. Do not go back and romanticize the time spent with your psychopath.

Eddie had me _thoroughly_ convinced that _I_ was the problem and that there was something inherently wrong with _me_. During several interactions he would infer that I was "deficient" without coming right out and saying so.

According to Eddie, I was "different" from practically the entire world because I placed value on such things as promptness, reliability, and trustworthiness. According to Eddie, my expectations were unrealistic and abnormal. He would also infer that I was lacking somehow in my understanding of things. If I reacted to something in a negative way, I was overreacting or "jealous." If I failed to react to something, I was "weak" and let others walk on me. By employing various techniques and mind games Eddie surreptitiously and systematically began to lay the foundational belief that I was atypical.

I was so confused and had come to believe, at least in part, that maybe he was right; perhaps there was something wrong with me. Because of this, I never spoke with anyone about the abuse I was receiving. This was the exact effect he was looking for.

I was having a very hard time identifying the real problem and felt too insecure to reach out.

However, one day I made a simple Google search: "Why do I feel so manipulated."

Wow! This simple question put into an on-line search brought forth a plethora of information about a different type of person I naively believed only existed in the movies - the psychopath. Suddenly I was plunged into greater clarity about the reality of what I was experiencing for the past four years and whom I was dealing with. I was not crazy; there was something terribly amiss with this man and the way I was being treated was far from normal.

I wish I could say that this was the end of my relationship with Eddie but it was not. Even though it was the <u>beginning</u> of my education into his twisted world, at this point it was merely head knowledge. With my heart I still believed at some level I could "reach" him and "heal" him of all his internal wounds that made him act the way he did. I wanted to believe that my great love for him would snap him out of it. I was in denial. My continued loyalty to him and misplaced desire to help him only resulted in his treatment of me to become worse.

You cannot fix the psychopath. Short of an act from God, psychopaths cannot be healed. There is no cure for psychopathy and currently no medication exists to treat it. Many healthcare professionals refuse to take psychopaths as patients because it is fruitless.

# Chapter Three - IN THE BEGINNING: "IDEALLY HIS"

Boy did I feel special! I had just received a promotion and started a new job where I met Eddie. He pursued me vigorously. He was always finding a reason to come to my office. We would have coffee and talk. Eventually, we would take walks during our lunch hour. We began our relationship as mere work acquaintances, and then we became friendly co-workers, and eventually so much more.

I ignored all the red flags, and surrendered my good sense to him. It was not until later that I learned that this phase is the idealization phase and as I pointed out in Chapter 2, also known as "love bombing."

In the beginning, Eddie asked me many questions and actually listened, which made it *seem* like he was *really* interested in me. Looking back I can see that he was not reciprocating by revealing equal amounts of information about himself. If this is happening to you, beware! Psychopaths gather information about you so they can reflect back to you precisely who you want them to be. If you need a knight in shining armor, they will be your Sir Lancelot! However, it is all a façade!

The psychopath will also study you to find out your insecurities, which he will later use to erode your self-confidence. Because he has assessed you, the psychopath is very in tuned to your emotions and takes advantage of this. You may even confuse this as his being the most caring and insightful man you have ever met. Perhaps he is, but nefariously so!

Eddie knew exactly what to say and do so that I would let my defenses down. He also managed to create an atmosphere where he was my "protector." He was able to make me believe that there were situations at work in which I was at some sort of risk and he appointed himself my guardian. This was done in order that I would feel indebted to him and give him my complete trust.

Although externally, a strong woman and accustomed to handling circumstances on my own, Eddie knew from prior conversations that internally I had a fear of failure and a need for approval. He would feed my insecurities by divulging negative words *allegedly* spoken about me by others, further undermining my sense of self-worth, and making me more dependent upon him and his acceptance of me. By doing so, he also gained the advantage he desired in order to continue his manipulation of various relationships in the workplace. For instance, on one of many stressful days at work, Eddie perceived my troubled state of mind and showed up at my home that evening with a vase full of flowers and a beautiful note singing my praises, in particular regarding my capability in carrying out the duties of my job. This led to a long detailed conversation about the circumstances of the day. When the timing was right for him, Eddie used the information I had shared with him while crying on his too willingly offered shoulder as a weapon against me in an effort to sabotage my credibility at work, while at the same time, ingratiating him with key administrative figures. Psychopaths gather information and store it in the dark recesses of their conniving mind and when it will benefit them, they pull it out and use it against you. You may be surprised because it may be years before they do so, but they are in no hurry. They have built a whole arsenal of weaponry ready to launch straight at your heart, reputation, relationships, and even possibly your bank account.

At first, I resisted spending time with Eddie, because he was still married. I refused to have, as he put it, "an innocent lunch" with him. He said his wife would not mind and he even offered to call her and ask her in front of me. I now realize that he was attempting to use me as a way of triangulation of his wife. Triangulation is a tactic that psychopaths use for a variety of reasons, including instilling jealousy or a sense of insecurity in one of the parties of the triangle, while making the other party feel very special, chosen. The third party (me at that time) often does not realize they are being used in the psychopath's scheme to hurt the other person. In hindsight, I see that at this point in our relationship, Eddie had me in the idealization stage and his wife in the devaluation stage. I said no to his offer for lunch. I tried to keep it friendly and all our contact was at work.

Granted, other men, even married men, have approached me in the past. The difference is that they respected my decision when I said no; however, when a psychopath has set his eyes on you, there is no such thing as "no."

Because control is so important to the psychopath, he may stalk you both in the initial stages of the psychopathic bond and in the end stages as well. The psychopath is a predator. He will study you. He will watch you. He will make a plan. When he is certain that his plan will work, he will pounce.

In the early stages of our work relationship, another co-worker asked me out to dinner. We agreed to meet at the local diner about a mile from work. I foolishly divulged all the details to Eddie, who showed up at the diner while we were there. He did not reveal his presence to us at the time; however, the next day he told me he saw us and described where we were sitting. Reflecting back, I see how creepy that was. At the time, however, I felt flattered that he would pursue me to that degree.

Eddie also admitted that he would wait at a gas station on a highway located on my commute to work in order to watch me go by, making it possible for him to follow me and arrive at work at the same time as I did.

One Saturday night, Eddie called me at home. He said he got my phone number off the work emergency phone number list. He apologized for using it and asked if it was OK. I politely answered that yes it was OK. This should have been a huge red flag for me because it overstepped so many boundaries on so many levels. At first, I thought he was calling about something work related; but that was not the case. He just chatted a little and then we ended the call; however, he continued to call me from different locations, each of which was getting closer and closer to my home. I was so naive. Why did I believe it was just a coincidence that he was now minutes away? Why did I not question how he knew where I lived?

Eventually, going against my better judgment, I agreed to meet with him at a secluded location a mere 10 minutes from my home. Eddie was so tender with me that night. This, of course, was all part of the seduction. Had he come on full force, I would have been appalled and he instinctively knew that. He just hugged me, looked into my eyes, and kissed my face, but never my lips. After about 17 years without having a man in my life, the hook was definitely in . . . deep. I was intoxicated with all of the attention that was being thrown at me

A maneuver that psychopaths use to secure a deeper bond with you is to create an impression that you are soul mates. You may share deeply personal information that actually was a part of your life experience. They are probably not reciprocating, but instead, take the information you have shared and reflect it back to you. This is called mirroring. Mirroring is a tactic that psychopaths use in order to make you feel as though you two share a special bond like no other. You feel a deep connection with them because you have been led to believe that you both have so much in common. In reality the psychopath is just taking information you have trustingly divulged to them as a means to gain a foothold into your heart. This shows just how callous a psychopath can be to take a traumatic event that you experienced and to capitalize on it for his own evil agenda.

The same evening I foolishly met Eddie at the secluded rendezvous, he told me about his wife cheating on him, making him a "victim" and subject to my sympathy. In a *very* warped way this "justified" our seeing each other although he was not yet formally divorced. It still shocks me that I involved myself with a man who was still married, regardless of his assurances that the marriage was over and the divorce was imminent. I regret doing so and am very remorseful for having allowed it. Reflecting back, I now remember that he told me about his wife's affairs <u>after</u> I had told him about my ex-husband having cheated on me. Therefore, his mirroring of also having a cheating spouse gave us a common bond. He told me other private things about their marriage and I never questioned whether they were actually true or not. I too told him personal things that I never shared with anyone else before.

Soon, Eddie began to show up unannounced at my home. This also is a means of control. I never knew when he was going to show up on my doorstep, which can be very disconcerting. Obviously, I did not have good boundaries to allow this to continue to happen. On numerous occasions I would come home and within a minute or two, he was at my front door. He lived well over an hour away and I believe he was either following me or waiting for me to come home. Once, towards the end of our relationship, when I was leaving an evening church service, I saw his car parked on a side street and sure enough he was at my front door within a few minutes. Stupidly, I did not confront him. I was angry about it but did not want to "embarrass" him.

Eddie said all the right things. He often brought flowers and gifts, which made it awkward to object to his uninvited visits. Some of these gifts were expensive and initially at least, I tried politely not to accept them, but he was very insistent. I mistook all of this attention as, "this man must *really* love me!" He helped me around the house a lot. I grew dependent upon him, which of course is what he intended. He sent countless texts and he called often. The more time I spent with Eddie, the less time I spent with others. This is a ploy the psychopath will use to isolate you from the influence of others in order that he can fully dominate you. You may not realize what is happening because the psychopath will make it so you will <u>want</u> to spend lots of time with him and will cleverly put distance between you and other people in your life.

At first, I could do no wrong. Eddie placed me high upon a pedestal. That is something I had never experienced before. For the most part, this made me feel great but sometimes uncomfortable. This probably went on for <u>at least</u> our first year together. I began to feel something new. I felt cherished and valuable. This was also part of the seduction. I would find out later what little value I actually had with him. Eddie also made me feel irreplaceable, when in fact little did I know he had my replacement already lined up. It was not long after I left my job that he initiated triangulation with my good friend and co-worker, Beth. He began to drop by her office and take walks with her at lunchtime. Later, he would speak vaguely about their interactions to me and was always sure to include hints of flirting. Of course, at the time I did not fully understand what was happening. I just knew that his interactions with her made me feel distressed. Again, exactly what he intended.

# Chapter Four – THE SLOW BOIL

I have heard the anecdote of the boiling frog as comparable to the relationship of the psychopath and his victim. The principle is that if a frog is placed in boiling water, it will jump out; however, it will not perceive the danger if placed in cold water that is slowly heated, and will be slowly cooked to death from the inside. It is a metaphor for the inability of people to react to or be aware of threats that occur gradually. I like to refer to this as the subtlety of the gradual. By the time you, the target, become aware that you are in danger, you may be too weak to get out of the pot! You are being cooked alive! Heck! You probably willingly jumped into that big pot because it was cleverly disguised as a refreshing pond by your prince who tempted you to join him as he reclined on the pad of a beautiful water lily. As the water heated and you began to sense you were in danger, you looked over just in time to see him turn into the toad he really is as he quickly exited the pot, warts and all.

Psychopaths are masters at positive and negative reinforcement. They are so cunning in the art of using these manipulations that you are not even aware of what is really happening. After all, they love you, right?

Psychopaths use these tactics to "condition" you to act and react in certain ways. Once the psychopath realizes that he has you exactly where he wants you with positive reinforcement, your loving psychopath will introduce you to something new that will leave your head spinning and your heart thoroughly confused. This is the beginning of the devaluation stage.

Although Eddie was never physically abusive of me, the mind games he cleverly launched were just as damaging. He carefully metered his attacks in small, almost undetectable, yet deadly doses. This was particularly true during our last year together.

Eddie did not call me names, but he did criticize and tease me often. For instance, he would pick me up and then would say, "Oh. You are a lot heavier than you used to be." Then he would add, "Just kidding." He would also say, "Everyone else in your family seems fine. It is just you . . ." and he would let his voice trail off. This was confusing considering prior to this time, he labeled me as being "perfect."

Eddie did not hit me but he would "playfully" pick me up or pin me down and say, "You know I would never hurt you right?" continuing to hold me down long enough to show who was in control.

Often, while hiking, Eddie would use my fear of heights by "pretending" to push me off a rock ledge or some other high point. He would then pull me back and laugh.

He loved to sneak up on me and scare me. He would hide in a dark room in the house and scare me as I entered the room. He would then laugh and say, "You are so predictable."

As heady as the idealization stage is for both the psychopath and his victim, it also requires a lot of time and energy and so the psychopath will eventually show his true colors. He wants to see how much abusive behavior you will tolerate without giving him the boot.

Just when you begin to question his conduct, the psychopath's inner radar kicks in and he will do something nice. As an effort to reel me back in, Eddie would take me out to dinner at our favorite restaurant and a romantic stroll along the riverfront afterward. On one occasion, toward the end of our relationship, Eddie showed up with a new expensive lounge chair for the patio. I did not want to accept it. I even asked him, "Why do you always show up with a gift when I am mad at you?" He seemed surprised that I asked, but never answered my question and he would not let me decline his unsolicited gift. By this point, you begin to doubt yourself and wonder if it may have been just your imagination or your own insecurities that made you distrust such a wonderful man. You are in denial. The devaluation will rear its ugly head again, becoming uglier each time it presents itself. The more unhealthy behavior you permit the more you will be devalued and diminished in the eyes of the psychopath. This is so ironic since he is the one behaving badly and when you object to his behavior, he will somehow turn the tables on you! You will not win with the psychopath.

One day you are the best thing since sliced bread and the next you are yesterday's news. The devaluation is usually gradual and intermingled with some positive reinforcement as well. Intuitively, the psychopath knows when to play which card. He enjoys playing with you. Moreover, he is probably not quite ready to discard you. You undoubtedly still feed him with whatever energy he thrives on getting from you and is most likely not yet ready to pounce on his new victim. Nonetheless, do not be fooled. The time and energy he once spent on you is now being lavished on someone else.

In order to keep you guessing and off-balance as to where you stand with him, the psychopath may initiate a period of silent treatment as a means of control. It also gives him time to be with his new victim. The silent treatment may last a few hours, a few days, a few weeks, or even longer. You will make yourself crazy wondering if you did something wrong. You may even reach out and apologize for something/anything you may possibly have done to offend him. He loves this.

I experienced the silent treatment more than once during my relationship with Eddie. Initially, they were relatively short periods of time but considering we spent enormous amounts of time together even a partial day without the usual phone call or text seemed out of the ordinary. Eventually the length of the silent treatment grew longer and longer.

One time in particular comes to mind. It was towards the end of our relationship and around the time I was becoming truly aware that the treatment I was receiving from Eddie was not normal. He sent me a text after about 5 weeks of no contact. This was the longest period of silent treatment thus far and came without warning (as usual) after my having made him a homemade dinner.

The night Eddie reinitiated contact was a cold wintery night around 8 p.m. and we were experiencing quite a blizzard.

The text read, "Thinking of you."

Unbelievably, I responded by asking him how he was and asking (in a nice way) what he was doing.

Not surprising was his vague response: "Not much; keeping busy."

I remembered that he had told me several weeks back that he was planning to drive down south to visit his sister for Thanksgiving and so I asked him if he was down south yet. He responded by asking me a question. I realized nothing had changed. He was still being vague and evasive and his text was nothing more than a fishing expedition to see if I was still a willing target. This was enough to snap me back into reality and I refused his offer to talk on the phone.

We did however end up communicating via e-mail later that evening, which ended with an e-mail from Eddie telling me that he loved me and I was his best friend regardless of what happened.

He then added, "<u>No need to respond to anything. In fact please don't because you'll probably ruin it.</u>"

Therefore, basically, he sent the e-mail because he wanted to have his say, without any response from me; and so, I did not respond and went to bed.

However, Eddie was not done. I was woken up around 2 a.m. with another text from him, "I just finished one bottle and am opening another," quickly followed by, "IF <u>YOU</u> HAD SPOKEN TO ME EARLIER, WE COULD HAVE AVOIDED ALL OF THIS!"

So now it was my fault that he was drunk! I rolled over and went back to sleep.

A few weeks after this incident I received the following text from Eddie, "Hello Melody. I was wondering if you wanted to have dinner tomorrow night. Now I promise, if you say no, it is ok. I promise it is ok. I don't want a long story or a bunch of haba haba - <u>just a yes or a no</u>. Thanks."

*(What? Am I even allowed to talk?)*

I am not sure why but I responded, "Well, I have church tomorrow night."

Eddie's response was simply, "OK. No problem."

*(That's it? There are other nights in a week!)*

I wait a few minutes but when I hear nothing, I text back, "Is there anything specific about tomorrow night?"

Eddie's response again was very brief, "No. I just wanted to see you."

Bewildered, I simply answered, "OK."

I had no further response from Eddie and there was no contact between us for quite awhile. I have no doubt that Eddie was fully aware that the night he asked me to dinner was a regular church night for me. It seemed as yet another test I had to pass; but of course, on his terms.

# Chapter Five – MIND GAMES

There is no end to the mind games that psychopaths play. After all, control is at the very core of their modus operandi. While in the idealization stage, the psychopath mainly manipulates you by pulling at your heartstrings; during the devaluation stage, they play with your psyche. First, the psychopath gains your trust and steals your heart. Then they are able to gain access to your thought processes and very subtly, over a period of time, using coercive persuasion will begin to systematically chip away at your core values and beliefs that make you uniquely you.

Psychopaths test their targets loyalty throughout the relationship. In the beginning, the tests are a means by which the psychopath can determine if you are a good target. By this, I mean he will put you through a series of tests to learn if you have boundaries and to ascertain if he will be able to successfully manipulate and exploit you. Although Eddie did not reveal this to me until well into our relationship, he tested my loyalty to him very early on. He explained that he purposefully divulged information to me about his supervisor and said that when the information did not make its way back to him, he knew he could trust me.

The tests begin very simply and superficially and may include the introduction of "unspoken rules." The psychopath covertly sets up these rules and we comply for fear of losing their approval. For example, Eddie told me that his ex-wife liked to walk around the house in slippers, making a scuffing noise that annoyed him. This set an unwritten rule I was not to wear slippers and scuff around the house and very subtly placed fear within my heart of possibly losing the "love" that I become dependent. Over time, as I unwittingly agreed with the suggested rules, they would become more serious and directed at my inner identity and core beliefs.

The psychopath will begin to plant the idea that he is no longer happy with you. You will find yourself doing whatever you can to regain the status you once had (or though you had) with your psychopath. You will wonder what you did to cause him to change; but he did not change. You are now actually beginning to see the real him. He knows he has you right where he wants you - confused and desperate. He will blame you for the change in his behavior and he will now begin to make requests of you. They may seem very simple non-important requests at first but don't be fooled. The psychopath will use this time to erode your self-image by getting you to do things that are out of character for you. In my opinion, this is the psychopath at the height of his control.

Now the psychopath specifically begins tailoring his requests of you to get you to turn your back on your own convictions. You will find yourself saying, "Yes" when you want to say,

"No". This will look different for each individual. For me this meant compromising some of my values and accepting more of his antics. I learned to keep quiet. It was easier. His tactics worked! I still did not like some of the things he was doing, but I was being conditioned to accept them.

Two of these tactics are similar and go hand in hand - minimization and rationalization.

Minimization is used when the psychopath wants to make you feel as though you are over-reacting should you question something they are doing. They put you on the defensive and claim you are "making a mountain out of a mole hill." They minimize what they are doing because they want you to "buy-in" and accept their unethical behavior so they can continue doing it without even needing to hide it.

Rationalization is nothing more than making excuses for inappropriate conduct. The psychopath wants to convince you that their behavior is either normal or justified. One reason they rationalize is so they can manage your impression of them while engaging in questionable behavior. They want to manage your impression of them because the persona that the psychopath has created is very important to them, especially in the early stages of the relationship. In the later stages of the relationship, they may not be so interested in managing your impression of them but still want to maintain the mask for others in your circle, some of whom he may be using for triangulation and some of whom he may have zeroed in on as their next target.

For example, Eddie thoroughly convinced my friend, Beth, who I referenced earlier as someone he began triangulating, that although he sometimes may tell small lies, when he says, "swear to God," he is telling the absolute truth. The reality is that he does not care about swearing to God! What he cares about is managing her impression of him. He knows that to swear to God that he is telling the truth while he is actually telling a lie would cross an unacceptable boundary for her; therefore, he has impressed upon her that this is a boundary he would never cross. He has studied her and is reflecting back to her what she wants to hear. I know that he has sworn to God and lied and he has sworn on his children's graves and lied.

Eddie used both minimization and rationalization often because he engaged in dishonest behavior often. For instance, if I caught him lying to someone other than myself, his excuse might be that it was for his or her own good or their own protection that he lied to them, thereby rationalizing his behavior. His job required that he be on call for any maintenance issues that might arise after hours. One frigid wintery evening while we were sitting watching television, Eddie received a call that there was a problem with the heat. This is something that he could adjust remotely from his phone. I overheard him politely tell the caller, "No problem. I will adjust the temperature right away." Eddie hung up the phone and continued to watch TV. Puzzled, I turned to him and asked if he were going to adjust the temperature. He replied, "No." When I pushed the issued, he retorted, "It's for their own good because if I adjust the heat, they will only complain later that they are too hot."

Although I now know of several instances where Eddie was engaging in unlawful behavior throughout our relationship, it was only toward the end that he did not bother to hide it from me. If I found out Eddie was involved in some minor unlawful conduct, he would say, "Everyone does it," both minimizing and rationalizing what he was doing.

Eddie actually told me that he was really intrigued by how certain evil, yet charismatic, leaders like Adolph Hitler and Jim Jones were able to get so many people to follow them, even though they were abusive. If we listen, the psychopath will occasionally give us BIG clues into who they really are!

Do not be fooled. Mind control is a very real and insidious mechanism that the psychopath has no twinge of guilt about using on his unsuspecting subject. They operate under the radar. Sam Vaknin talks about this in one of his YouTube videos:

https://www.youtube.com/watch?v=Va32SSPWa1w

The target is unsure of the abuse because the abuse is intermingled with words of love, making it difficult to label the abuse as abuse. Targets of this sort of abuse begin to doubt their own sanity. Personally, I was so confused and felt so alone. I did not know whom I should turn to.

You probably have heard of the expression The Stockholm Syndrome. The term originated from an incident in Stockholm, Sweden where a bank robbery occurred and a phenomenon took place in which the hostages defended their captors at the end of the ordeal because they had become emotionally attached to them. The Stockholm Syndrome is a form of traumatic bonding.

Traumatic bonding occurs as a result of ongoing abuse in which there are cycles of intermittent reinforcement of reward and punishment. This creates a powerful emotional bond between the aggressor and the victim. It is a potent attachment and the psychopath knows it! It is very difficult to break free from, especially when the psychopath employs hovering.

Hovering is a technique in which the psychopath will try to suck you back into the relationship. This brings anxiety to my soul as I remember the numerous times I tried to walk away from Eddie but to no avail. Every time I tried to make a break, he would reinitiate the idealization stage. I tried to escape the hold he had on me; but he would always show up with tears in his eyes and some gift, favor, or promise just for me. He simply would not take no for an answer!

Another technique of psychological manipulation is gaslighting. Psychopaths love to employ gaslighting because it can make you, the victim, believe you are losing your mind. It may come in the way of a conversation you had that they say never happened. When this occurs often enough, the person being gaslighted begins to believe that they cannot trust their own memory. Another way the psychopath uses gaslighting is by deliberately making subtle changes to your environment such as moving a picture from one spot to another or moving your keys from the spot you left them.

I had a situation after our break-up where I believe Eddie was breaking into my car (he had a spare key) and changing the position of various dials on my dashboard. At first, I thought, I must have been mistaken as to what temperature or airflow I had left my car at when I went to work. It became so bothersome that I began to take a picture of the control dials before I exited my car. Sure enough, when I came back at the end of the day, they were different. This did not occur every day but was sporadic. I bought a mini motion-detector camera and placed it out of view in the front of my car. At least I thought it was out of view. Eddie is very familiar with things such as hidden cameras and recorders and can spot them from a mile away. I knew this, but did the best I could; however, I could never seem to get a recording after I left the car, not even of me getting back into the car. Obviously, the motion detection component was not working properly due to manufacturer defect or possibly tampering.

Do not bother trying to expose the psychopath's gaslighting. They will make it appear as though you are "losing it."

Unfortunately, others will believe this because the psychopath, who is always one-step ahead, has already planted those negative ideas about you.

# Chapter Six – PANTS ON FIRE!

*Liar, Liar! Pants on Fire!*
*I don't care, I don't care. I can buy another pair!*

Vagueness, lies and lies of omission are the only way psychopaths communicate. The psychopath can look you right in the eye and tell you a bold face lie because it is second nature to them. It does not matter how insignificant the issue may be, the psychopath just seems to delight in getting one over on you.

The lies Eddie told were endless. To this day, I am still unsure of what, if any, was actual truth. Eddie "admitted" to me that he lied under oath during a workplace arbitration hearing. This was after I had resigned from my position and was attempting to get away from him. He stopped by to see me after work and he announced that there was a hearing earlier that day and that he lied under oath in order to "protect me." Until this point, I did not know about the hearing and I certainly would never have asked him to lie! I would have no reason to do so. When I stated this to him, his whole demeanor changed and he threatened, "Next time you will be on your own." To this day, I am still uncertain if he actually did lie under oath or merely told me he lied in order that I would feel indebted to him for his "protection."

The psychopath may pretend they are being upfront with you about plans or situations but will leave out important information while flooding you with many useless details.

This brings me to a maneuver that psychopaths use which has been appropriately named "future-faking". The psychopath makes promises to you that he has no intention of keeping, purposefully planting a seed of false hope into your trusting heart. This shows how unscrupulous the psychopath really is. The psychopath has studied you. He knows your heart's desire and understands exactly what you want from him but he does not intend to give it to you. He alludes giving it to you sometime in the future when the "timing is right"; but that day never comes. This may be the hope of getting married or maybe having a baby together. In my case, I so desperately wanted Eddie to be a Godly man, to come to church, and for us to one day get married. Initially, he did come to church and commented that he could see himself doing so in the long-run, but that promise dwindled out. He also had me believe that we would be married in the future. We talked about what kind of wedding we wanted and even drove around looking at houses together. Although I told Eddie that I wanted to meet his family, the four years we were together it never happened. He knew meeting his parents was important to me since I lost both of mine at a young age, but the timing was never right for him.

Another tactic Eddie used <u>a lot</u> was to be EXTREMELY evasive. He never gave a straight answer about anything. This was especially true towards the end of our relationship. He liked to keep me guessing . . . about everything. For instance, after a night out Eddie would kiss me and say, "See you next time." He did not say, "I'll call you tomorrow," or even, "Let's get together again on Thursday." He knew I am the type of person that needs to plan. He also knew that I needed assurance of his commitment to me. Therefore, he was certain not to give it, leaving me to play the old schoolgirl game of picking the petals off the daisy reciting, "He loves me, he loves me not." If you take anything from this book, please remember, you should never have to second guess where you stand with someone who professes to love and care for you!

A typical conversation and another example of his evasiveness came just prior to our final break-up and went as follows, with me initiating the conversation:

"Your son is getting married soon, right?"

"Yea, I guess."

"You guess? Well, is he getting married or not?"

"He is."

"When?"

"Sometime this summer, I guess."

"Aren't you going? Don't you know when it is?"

"I don't know. I just go where and when they tell me."

Now that is a joke! He does not take orders from anyone!

Because the old way of relating with your psychopath has ended, you will begin to feel like you are walking on eggshells. Eddie used to say that I made him feel as though he were walking on eggshells. The psychopath will accuse you of doing things that they are actually doing. Once you realize this, it is a pretty good way of knowing what they are doing! If they accuse you of lying, they are probably lying. If they accuse you of cheating, you can bet they are cheating. Unfortunately, for me this realization came after the break-up of our relationship.

Eventually you will realize that you are sad more often than happy. You will wake up and understand that your dream man has become your worst nightmare and you are being boiled alive from the inside out.

For me, it was around this time that the next stage was introduced. If they can no longer dominate you, they will discard you.

# Chapter Seven - PRE-DISCARD/ DISCARD

Psychopaths will not discard until they are certain they are done with you. Nor will psychopaths discard until they have secured a new victim. Psychopaths will continue the abusive cycle of idealization, devaluation, and discard over and over again as long as you let them. They like to hover to see if they can come back for one more bite of you. Often, the psychopath will keep you in their life, but on the sidelines, just in case they want to come back and take a nibble. You are no longer the main course but tasty nonetheless.

Sometimes Eddie would bring up the name of someone at work or the gym and casually tell a story of "innocent" flirtation in order to stir up feelings of insecurity. This was done to keep me guessing as to where I stood with him. If I reacted, he would turn the tables on me and accuse me of being insecure and jealous. After quite a few rounds of this over a period of time, I decided to tell Eddie that I did not want to hear it. When I did, he simply stated matter-of-factly, "Then I'll stop telling you." This of course was a veiled threat. He did not say, it would not continue. He merely "agreed" to keep me in the dark. Another thing he began to do was strategically place two empty cups of coffee in his car for me to see, planting the idea that someone other than me had been in his car. So many tactics all thrown into one bag! By this time, though, I did not take the bait. I knew better. Whether another woman was in the car with him or he was trying to instill jealousy in me, was quickly becoming irrelevant.

Towards the end of our relationship Eddie asked me to go with him to pick out new furniture for his home and then to get a bite to eat. Almost the entire time we were out he ignored me and was on the phone with at least one of his triangulating targets. He was being purposefully rude and was baiting me. Later when he brought me home, he cruelly remarked, "That was fun. I enjoyed messing with you."

Another way the psychopath may use triangulation is by involving a third party to corroborate their opinions. He will manage to get the third party to buy into their lies and then use them to gang up on you. The third party is usually oblivious to the fact that the psychopath is using them to hurt you.

The psychopath may also triangulate by splitting the two other parts of the triangle by pitting them against each other, smearing one against the other and vise versa. This way, each party believes they have a "special" relationship with the psychopath, but it also puts a wall between them. At this point, the psychopath does not want them talking and comparing notes! Both parties are still of use to him.

The night Eddie and I were out shopping for new furniture we also stopped at the Christmas Tree Shop. Eddie told me that when he was in Beth's office, he accidentally broke the mug I had given her as a parting gift when I resigned and he wanted to buy her a new one. The broken mug was very cute and had a funny quote that was very apropos considering the confidential nature of our jobs. It said, "We will be friends forever. You know too much." We looked around and finally agreed on one with this quote, "Lord, put your arm around my shoulder and your hand over my mouth." This was also appropriate for Beth who sometimes has a hard time keeping her thoughts to herself.

Curiously, a few days later, Eddie came to my house to show me some nick-knacks he had purchased. In the bag was a beautiful mug with the word, "Hope." When I asked Eddie about it he replied that he did not mean to bring it in the house and that the mug was for Beth. I remember being taken aback by this. I had a feeling of angst in the pit of my stomach and quietly wondered, *"Really? But you already purchased a mug for her. What are you 'hoping' for with Beth?"*

A few evenings later, I invited Eddie to my grandson's birthday party. While driving there, Beth called to thank me for the mug, stating the quote on it was perfect for her. I was surprised that Eddie told her the mug was from me because he paid for it and claimed he was buying it for her because he broke the original mug. I (foolishly) went along and pretended it was from me and I never asked about the other (Hope) mug. As we were pulling into my daughter's driveway, Beth suddenly realized that I was not alone and she asked, "Is Eddie with you?" I said "Yes." Beth offered a quick good-bye and hung up. Eddie then asked me, "Did she call you from her cell phone?" I replied, "Yes. Why?" He did not answer me but instead called Beth. I heard him laughingly tell Beth, "We're through. OK. I'm hurt. I'm hurt. It's over." He laughed and when he hung up I ask him what that was all about and he said, "Oh nothing." In addition, his little tee-hee's and ha-ha's with her were going on in my daughter's driveway as she stood in the doorway with my grandchildren patiently waiting for us to come inside. Argghh!

Finally, the psychopath who is really done with you will use this third party (or group of people) to "confide in" about how crazy you are and how hard he tried to help you and stay in the relationship with you. One of these confidants will undeniably be the new you. Lucky them!

Lucky me! Eddie used all of these triangulation techniques on me. Aside from questioning my own sanity, I think this may have been the most hurtful part of this whole experience. He used my friends in his ploy to bring me down. Of course, he cleverly disguised his tactic so that none of them understood what he was really doing. Camouflaging his insults of me as concern for me, he planted negative seeds in their minds disguised as flattery and/or concern. He made comments such as, "I love her dearly. If only she wouldn't push her religion on me"; "I don't know why she is so jealous of our friendship. I'm glad you aren't jealous like that"; "I don't understand why she just broke it off with me for no reason"; "She has issues." My friends were conned into believing that he was the victim when he was actually the perpetrator. How ironic. How hurtful. The final blow is that he has now taken my friends from me and my reputation and dignity to boot.

If this is happening, do not try to defend yourself because the more you do, somehow the crazier you look and therefore you are just validating the picture the psychopath has painted of you. It is so frustrating because the psychopath is still wearing his charismatic good guy mask to everyone else. You know the truth but few would believe you and you would be wasting your energy.

Shortly after my relationship with Eddie came to an end, I seriously contemplated confronting my friend with the truth; however, it only took a few minutes into a casual conversation that I realized that this would be a big mistake. Almost every word out of her mouth, sounded as though Eddie were talking. It was too late! He had already planted ideas in her mind and she was his puppet!

I now look back and remember how Eddied planted negative seeds in my mind regarding his ex-wife and other women as well. I never would have believed any of them had they approached me at the time.

Initially, when I still believed that I held the unrivaled position of soul mate, it really stung when the realization hit home that someone else now ranked higher than I did! I remember experiencing a flood of emotions. As each wave came crashing down, it brought with it a new and surprising response. Fear, anger, and extreme jealousy roused up from within, accompanied by despondency, incited by my old "friend" rejection. If this is happening to you, please do not fret; one day the realization that you have been replaced will bring a new emotion – relief!

Around the same time I became aware that Eddie was using triangulation, his mask slipped several times. I still am not sure if he consciously allowed this or he just did not care anymore. Whatever the case, it was frightening to behold.

A particular incident occurred at my home and I believe it was the last time Eddie was in my house. He stopped by after work and was telling me about a conversation he had with one of my female friends at work. The conversation revolved around the fact that they were both overweight at some point in their life and Eddie said that they showed each other pictures of themselves during that time period. This was surprising to me since he very rarely made himself vulnerable to anyone; but of course, he was using the mirroring technique with her. (Yet another friend he was triangulating.) I asked to see the picture and he obliged. When he wanted it back, I teased him and did not release it right away. His whole demeanor changed and as he forcefully grabbed the picture out of my hand he threatened, "You will find pictures of yourself plastered all over the internet in unflattering 'angles'." This was frightening because I knew he meant what he said but I did not know as to what pictures he could possibly be referring. I know first-hand that Eddie secretly records people. He is expert at it. I know that he has secretly recorded some of my phone conversations because of information he later had that he could not have gotten any other way. My mind was racing. Did Eddie also videotape me without my knowledge? Did he have a camera hidden somewhere in my home? The very thought of this has to be every woman's worst nightmare and now it was mine!

Although by then I knew the truth of what he is, to actually witness the coldness of his heart towards me was like having a bucket of ice dumped on me. I guess that is what I needed to turn tail and run. I finally reached out to family who helped me get the professional help I needed.

I broke it off with Eddie first and made it clear that I did not want any contact with him. I guess this was fine with him because this was the first time after breaking up with him that he did not immediately try to reinitiate the idealization stage. I am sure he was thinking that I did him a favor by ending it. He had moved on to his next victim, who as I mentioned before had been a dear friend. I felt I would probably be okay as long as I did not interfere with his new relationship with her, which would be unlikely anyway because he was keeping the two of us apart by cunningly pitting us against each other.

It took a while for the brainwashing affects to wear off. At first, I was even afraid to write down any of my thoughts. That is how sinister his work had been. I believed that he might somehow come into my house and read what I wrote and I would pay dearly for it. Although I had the locks changed, I was still concerned about him gaining entry. A few weeks before the final incident, Eddie and I were walking out of my home, getting into our individual cars, going our separate ways. We soon realized that he forgot his keys inside on the kitchen counter. I laughed and said, I guess you now have to come with me to the evening church service. I can still hear Eddie's sarcastic reply, "You don't think I haven't already made copies of your keys?" That was chilling. I had previously offered him keys but he refused them, stating that he didn't feel right taking a key to my home, but he then secretly made one!

Eddie was very clear when he expressed to me that he would get revenge against anyone who crossed him and he would ensure no one could ever possibly find out that it was he. Eddie indicated that he had done this in the past and he explained that one means he used for retribution was by messing with the persons' car.

Curiously, in the months post break-up I had two out of the ordinary "mishaps" with my car.

The first happened when the oil in my car suddenly and completely drained. There was a note on my windshield saying to be careful because they (the writer of the note) would hate to find me dead on the road somewhere. The handwriting on the note, while not exact, had elements similar to Eddie's handwriting.

The second mishap was when the brakes on my car, without any warning, suddenly failed. Of course, I have no way of proving that Eddie was responsible for either.

I never would have believed it in the beginning of our relationship, but I now know he is very dangerous. Aside from the post break-up car situations, I even believe that at one point during our relationship, Eddie had a plan to kill me. To explain, I need to give some background.

Eddie never invited me to his home. One day, a few years into our relationship, I called him and invited myself over. Since he lives about an hour and a half away and in a secluded wooded area, we agreed that I would meet him in the parking lot of a shopping mall at about the halfway point, where I would leave my car. After a walk around his property, we sat down on his front porch where he suddenly announced, almost as though he were pondering aloud, "I could kill you and nobody would know." I replied, "What?" He continued, "Nobody knows you are here. Your car is not anywhere near here. I could kill you and bury you over there," pointing to a garden area on the side of his house.

After this, but not too long before our relationship ended, Eddie called and asked if he could take me out to dinner to a restaurant that was close to where his family and ex-wife lived. This was odd and out of character for him, but desperate for his attention, I agreed. After dinner he said he wanted to "show me something." We drove awhile and he pointed out his ex-wife's house and remarked that we might see her because she often takes walks down this road. My instinct kicked in and I stupidly blurted, "So are you two planning on killing me?" Any normal person would have either laughed or replied with a denial of any intention of foul play and would say so immediately to alleviate any fear. Unbelievably, he did not respond at all, leaving me to wonder what exactly his intentions were. He drove down the hill and pulled over to a secluded wooded area with a small dirt path. He again reiterated that he wanted to "show me something." It was dusk and I was unsure what was going on but at his insistence, I followed him into the woods. I know! I know! Please remember that I was still holding on to the hope that the man I fell in love with and whom I believed loved me was still there inside somewhere. Full of dread, my heart thumped with each step I took, anxious about what might be waiting for me in the woods. After a somewhat short walk in partial darkness, I heard running water. We came to an area overlooking a waterfall with a stream and rocks at the bottom. I felt afraid. Eddie's demeanor and secretiveness were scaring me. He stood behind me and penned me in with his strong arms, leaning over the meager railing without ever saying a word. I was confused as to why we were there. After several minutes, I told him that I wanted to go, but he was reluctant to do so, and did not release his hold on me. It seemed as though he was biding his time, waiting for someone to show up or trying to decide whether to take some sort of action. Eventually I said I had to use the bathroom and for some reason, he finally relented. As we got into his car, another car with three young men pulled up, which appeared as if they were up to no good because it was getting dark and we were in a secluded area. At the time, this made me wonder if they were somehow part of an evil plot of Eddie's but arrived too late to go forward with it as we were no longer in the woods. Considering this further, I would have to conclude that Eddie would not include others in his scheme because he would be careful not to have anyone to point the finger at him. I do not know what Eddie had planned for that evening, but I know it was not good.

I also believe that there was a point Eddie considered killing his then wife. He told me that he had rented a wood chipper to reduce some of the trees on his property and he laughingly said he told his wife that she had better behave during the divorce or she would end up in the chipper. (*I have to wonder if she was laughing at the time.*) On another occasion, out-of-the-blue, he announced that he found out that the best way to dispose of a body through a wood chipper would be to freeze the body first. He then added that this would require getting a big freezer. Months later as we were sitting watching TV, I mentioned that a new show was coming on called, "How to Get Away with Murder." He responded, "I already know how" but then quickly added, "Just kidding." Besides all of this, an acquaintance of mine who had a tree cutting business was selling a wood chipper and Eddie was so excited about it and insisted that he "needed it" and he wanted me to secure a deal for him. Remembering back on his earlier comments about his wife, I gave a resounding, "No!"

It is so challenging to express sufficiently the depth and intensity of the exploitation and mind control that took place. Someone reading this book that has not personally experienced being in the grip of a psychopath may have a difficult time understanding how a grown woman could not only get herself mixed up with such a person, but also stay with them for so long. I am guessing, however, that because you have chosen to read this book, you do understand.

Eventually I got out from under Eddie's manipulation and I could think clearly for the first time in long time. This took about three months of no contact and weekly visits with a licensed therapist. Initially, I was ashamed that I let this happen. Then I became very angry, first with myself and then with him; but after I processed all of that hurt and anger I found myself again.

What's more, you can too! First, it is important that you recognize the psychopath for who he really is . . . not who you want him to be. Second, understand that you do have control of your life and your future. Third, accept the fact you must initiate the necessary changes in order to become free. After all, the spider is not going to stop his ways and suddenly help you find your way out of his web.

When you begin to take these vital steps, you will find yourself again and you will love and respect yourself enough to look before leaping into a relationship. You will care enough about yourself, your life and your future never again to allow the sort of abuse you have been accepting. You will be free to explore and learn what healthy boundaries are and how you can successfully employ them.

Once you have extricated yourself from the psychopath's control, you will think more clearly and become strong enough so that if the psychopath tries to re-enter your life (and they usually do) you will recognize it for what it is and act accordingly. Author Sam Vaknin calls this re-idealization. The psychopath's supply is running dry and so he re-idealizes you in his mind with the ultimate plan to begin the process with you all over again. Do not be flattered when he reappears. Understand that he only came back hoping that you are still willing to be his victim.

Oddly enough, a few days ago at this writing, after 15 months of no contact, Eddie did just that. I could see that the phone number of the person calling me was blocked but I picked up the phone anyway. "Hello?" Eddie was on the other end of the line. I have to admit I was a little stunned at hearing his voice again. He proceeded to talk as though nothing had happened. He spoke almost non-stop and mentioned that the past year had been very difficult for him because his mother had passed away and he had been diagnosed with cancer. He continued on with some of the details but ended with saying that he was now feeling much better. After quietly listening, I responded very flatly, "I'm glad you are feeling better. I have to go. Good Bye" and I quickly ended the call without giving him an opportunity to respond. I wish however, that I had just hung up the moment I heard his voice. It is clear that by blocking his identity on caller ID he intended to catch me off guard and continue to try to deceive and manipulate me.

Zero contact is essential to your freedom. You will not be able to come out of the fog if you are still under the influence of the one who is manipulating you. If contact is necessary for legal reasons, then cold, flat, and disengaging answers are best. If contact occurs accidentally as it did for me, then act indifferent, because to show any emotion, whether positive or negative feeds the psychopath and keeps him engaged.

Earlier I said you could not win with a psychopath. What I meant was you could not win at their games. You can win big, however, by leaving the relationship and by initiating and maintaining no contact.

# FINAL THOUGHTS

You have heard my story. I hope that you now believe that you are not alone and that the problem is not you. I have heard it explained this way: You merely loved the person you thought he was and believed that you were truly loved back. Yes, you ignored some red flags. Forgive yourself and resolve that you will listen to your gut instinct in the future.

You should not attempt this alone. It is such a confusing time and so easy to be drawn back in. Prior to obtaining professional help, I was drawn back into the relationship many times.

So please do not hesitate to seek professional help. A therapist will assist you in sorting through your emotions, reasons why this happened, and support you as you make your way to healthier clearer thinking. You will then be better equipped to recognize and avoid future abusive relationships. If anything, having an outside objective person to validate what you experienced will be invaluable to your self-esteem and psyche. Do not minimize what happened to you. Many of us have suffered Post-Traumatic Stress Disorder from our experience with a psychopath and required professional help. It is often needed to gain and keep your freedom. The long-term and insidious effects of mind control more than likely require this level of intervention.

It was important for me to have help from someone who understood the spiritual struggle I was in as well and so, I recruited the help of a licensed counselor who is a Christian. I also relied on the Bible and the Holy Spirit to guide me. You may also want to seek spiritual counseling, if appropriate for you.

Below are additional resources that I found helpful.

Websites:

>https://www.psychopathfree.com/

>http://outofthefog.website

Books:

>Psychopath Free by Jackson MacKenzie

>How Many Lies Are Too Many by Victoria Summit

>Malignant Self Love by Sam Vaknin

>Sheep in Wolves Clothing by George K. Simon

I mentioned initiating and maintaining no contact. This is a method designed to help individuals who are in abusive relationships remain free from those who are oppressing them. Do an internet search on "No Contact Rule." It may save your life. My going no contact was probably not as complicated as it would be for others who are living with, married to, or share children and property with a psychopath. If you have additional entanglements which make it necessary to have some contact, never meet alone and always in a neutral public place. Since this was not the case for me, I refer you to others who did and still successfully gained a reasonable degree of no contact. Visit the sites listed above or ideally seek professional help.

Here is my invitation to you. Please, believe in yourself again. I believe in you!

In case you are curious as to how I chose my pen name, Melody, it was for the simple and wonderful reason that ever since I have come out from under the oppressor's control, I have a new song in my heart and its' melody is one of freedom.

You too can be free.

Come out of that dark place and join me in the marvelous light. You will never regret it. Like me, you will one day be able to look back at this time and no longer feel pain but relief as you are now free to be all you were meant to be.

# TACTICS THE PSYCHOPATH USES ALONG WITH A BRIEF DESCRIPTION

These are tools the psychopath employs to manipulate you and to maintain control (Remember, they employ these tactics very purposefully)

**Blaming** - If you had done (fill in the blank) we could have avoided this.

**Denial** – "Who me?" They put you on the defensive. How dare you! Now you feel guilty.

**Evasiveness** – You will notice that the psychopath does not give a straight answer to even the simplest question. They just change the topic or turn your question to them into a question for you.

**Feigning Ignorance** – Plays dumb. "I have no idea what you are talking about." (Yes they do know!)

**Feigning Innocence** – Look of surprise. Pretends that whatever the offense is, it was unintentional.

**Future Faking** – The Psychopath makes promises about the future they have no intention of keeping.

**Gaslighting** – Emotional and psychological abuse to create doubt in the victims mind. (Example: You and the psychopath make plans to go see a movie the next evening but when the time comes, the psychopath says that conversation never happened.)

**Guilt Tripping** – Makes you believe you are to blame by using your good conscience against you. This keeps you submissive. On the other hand, they will never apologize for anything.

**Hovering** – The psychopath returns to the courting stage to manipulate you back into the relationship, often showing up in unexpected places.

**Intimidation** – This can include veiled threats ("If you ever did that to me I would –fill in the blank"); sneaking up on you; excessive tickling; holding you down "playfully"; pounding on the table; etc.

**Lies** – A psychopath will lie about everything and anything. It comes 100% naturally to them. Sometimes they will tell a flat out lie; sometimes their lie will have a grain of truth in it; sometimes they lie by omitting important facts.

**Love Bombing** – A technique used during the idealization stage of the psychopathic bond in which the psychopath inundates you with excessive amounts of attention, excessive flattery and gifts.

**Minimization** – They want to make you feel like you are over-reacting. "You are making a mountain out of a mole hill." It puts you on the defensive. They want you to "buy-in" and accept their improper behavior.

**Mirroring** – The psychopath studies you and becomes your mirror image – thus your soul mate.

**Playing the Servant or Savior Role** – Pretends to work on your behalf so that you will owe them and/or be dependent upon them.

**Playing the Victim** – They do this to evoke compassion.

**Rationalization**- This is how they excuse inappropriate behavior. Again, they want to convince you that their behavior is either normal or justified. They also use it to manage your impression of them.

**Shaming** – subtle sarcasm; putdowns; instills the belief that there is something unsuitable with you.

**Showing Anger** – To shock you into submission; Deliberate.

**Triangulation** –The Psychopath will recruit a third party for various reasons including to instill jealousy; to begin a smear campaign; to have the third party act as a go-between – they often do not realize they are being used; or for fun because the third party is their new target.

**Vagueness** – Psychopaths are purposefully vague to keep you guessing and to make you feel unsure of where you stand with them. They have all the control. They will give you unimportant information so it appears they are above board but leave out essential details.

# STAGES OF THE PSYCHOPATHIC BOND

**Stage One – Idealization:** The first stage of the psychopath cycle. The Psychopath lures you in with their charm and attention. They shower you with excessive flattery and attention. You can do no wrong. You are their "soul mate."

**Stage Two – Devaluation:** The second stage of the psychopath cycle. The Psychopath starts pulling away. He will give you small doses of positive reinforcement to keep you on the hook. He will continually push the boundaries of unacceptable behavior and as you accept the behavior he becomes less interested in you. You will be thoroughly confused as to what is really happening.

**Stage Three – Discard:** The final stage of the psychopath cycle. They have taken everything from you and have no use for you any longer and so they discard you. This is usually accompanied by a smear campaign against you. They have moved on to their next target.

www.ingramcontent.com/pod-product-compliance
Lightning Source LLC
Chambersburg PA
CBHW062105280526
45788CB00003B/1353